I PLEDGE ALLEGIANCE

I PLEDGE ALLEGIANCE

Politics for the citizens of heaven

STEPHEN DAVEY

CHARITY HOUSE

I Pledge Allegiance

ISBN: 0-9776641-1-2

Author: Stephen Davey
Cover Design and Text Layout: Shannon Brown, Advance Graphics (www.advancegraphics.us)

CONTENTS

Foreword

Whether through the media or at public gatherings, believers are besieged by religious and social voices to protect their rights through political activism. We are admonished to write letters, make phone calls, and send e-mails imploring our politicians to defend our cause. Those who demand our involvement often build their platform through misinterpreted and misapplied Scripture. Believers are convinced they have a moral obligation to get involved, and those who don't join are accused of lacking concern for their family, church, and nation.

Have you ever wondered where your obligation lies? Are you confused about whether your role as a citizen conflicts with that as a church member? What does the Bible really teach about our responsibility to the local and national authorities? Does it say anything at all? Thankfully, Scripture is not silent on this very important issue; however, the words and actions of Jesus and His apostles have been twisted and misused to support personal and political agendas.

In this book, Dr. Stephen Davey expounds the Word of God with insight and depth, shedding new light on our purpose as born-again Christians in the world arena. With your Bible in hand, I welcome you to *I Pledge Allegiance*.

Dr. Lowell Davey

President of the Bible Broadcasting Network

✝

Every person is to be in subjection to the

governing authorities. For there is no authority

except from God, and those which exist are

established by God.

Chapter 1

MISSING THE MARK

Romans 13:1

The opening lines of the Pledge of Allegiance were written in 1892 by Francis Bellamy, a Baptist minister. Bellamy was heavily influenced by a relative who had written that utopia within any society was possible, given the dedication and unity of mankind.

He wrote the original pledge to celebrate the anniversary of Columbus' arrival in the Americas. It was published in a children's magazine and was intended to stress the unity of the states as it declared,

> *I pledge allegiance to my Flag,*
> *and the Republic for which it stands;*
> *one Nation indivisible,*
> *with Liberty and Justice for all.*

Twenty-five years later, there was growing concern about the many immigrants who would not know what was meant by "my Flag." In 1923, the wording was added to the beginning line, "I pledge allegiance to the Flag of the United States." One year later "of America" was added, the pledge now reading,

> *I pledge allegiance to the Flag*
> *of the United States of America,*
> *and to the Republic for which it stands;*
> *one Nation indivisible,*
> *with Liberty and Justice for all.*

Thirty years later, in an attempt to differentiate America, with its belief in a Creator, from the spreading communism and atheism of other nations, the words "under God" were included. After these words were ratified, President Dwight D. Eisenhower wrote, "From this day forward, the millions of our school children will daily proclaim in every city and town, every village and schoolhouse, this...patriotic oath and public prayer." Note those last words—the Pledge of Allegiance was unapologetically conceived as a *prayer*.

Now, fifty years after Eisenhower applauded the new pledge, it is becoming the center of a growing controversy.

The Pledge of Allegiance is *undeniably* an oath and a confession; a public prayer; a declaration of the sovereignty of God.

For this reason Michael Newdow, the atheist father of a third grader, challenged the state of California for allowing a teacher to lead his daughter's class in the Pledge of Allegiance. The 9th U.S. Circuit Court of Appeals agreed with him and declared such an act unconstitutional.

However, in June of 2004, the Supreme Court reversed that decision. In the process, the Supreme Court sidestepped the real issue; they merely overruled the lower court because they held that the father had no right to speak for his daughter since he was presently involved in a custody dispute over her with his former wife. The Court rather neatly begged off on addressing the weightier issue of church and state as it relates to the Pledge of Allegiance.

There is little doubt that we are living in days of great alarm concerning issues of church and state.

How are we to respond to these issues? What do the apostles mean when they tell us to live in quietness (1 Timothy 2:1–2), to be submissive to rulers and authorities (Titus 3:1), and to be subject to every human institution, including the emperor and governors (1 Peter 2:13–14)? What does Paul mean when he writes in Romans 13:1,

Every person is to be in subjection to the governing authorities. For there is no authority except from God, and those which exist are established by God.

What does this text imply about the role and authority of the government and the role and authority of the church? How do the state and the church live in co-existence? Are there unique roles for each? Is the Apostle Paul saying that the government of Nero was ordained by God? How do we apply this perspective in the twenty-first century?

Before we get to the answers, it is important to raise the questions. In fact, I expect to trouble you; to provoke your critical thinking faculties to ask questions about the contemporary church age that we live in.

I will never forget my former professor Howard Hendricks saying in class one day, "In every generation, the church at large has missed the mark somewhere." He then pointed his finger at us and asked, "Do *you* know where it is missing the mark today?"

One of the critical areas in which the church is presently missing the mark is in its relationship to government. Specifically, in its desire for political influence to stem the tide of immorality and evil.

Frankly, we have arrived at a point in our country's history where both church and state are confused on this issue.

The state is deeply confused over its relationship with the church. What has become known as the wall of separation between church and state has nothing to do with our founding fathers' intentions.

Our founding fathers intended to create protection for the church from state-imposed religion. Instead of protecting the church from the state, the first amendment is presently interpreted to pull the drain and wash away the influence of the church; to slowly rid culture of any religious expression. The separation of church and state has become the separation of state *from* the church; the separation of state *from* God.

Today, that same ammendment is being twisted to defend the right to do all manner of things. One elementary school girl in Virginia was told to stop reading her Bible on a school bus because it violated the separation of church and state. In Decatur, Illinois, a primary school teacher who discovered the word *God* in a phonics textbook was able to order his seven-year-olds to color over it so that it could not be seen.

You now can use the constitution to defend someone's right to look at pornography in the locker room, but not the Bible in a classroom. You have the right to use profanity, but not the right to mention God respectfully.

The only thing that ever brings any change in this politically correct culture which intentionally shuns God is a war or an act of terrorism. Then, suddenly, leaders on both sides of the aisle, from the most powerful to the least influential are calling on America to pray and assuring grieving loved ones that they are in our prayers.

The state is certainly confused about its response and its relationship to the church.

There is, unfortunately, a greater problem. The greater problem is not the degradation of our society that does not love God or the Bible. The greater danger is not the erosion of values, the desire of our country to strike God from textbooks and courthouses, or even our citizens' interest in becoming the second city of Sodom. Greater than the degradation of society's fall from grace into ever-increasing evil is the *distraction* of the church and the *diversion* of the church's resources, manpower, and objectives.

The greater problem is a church which has left its first love; the church that believes making disciples one at a time is too slow, which would suggest that Jesus Christ was a failure to have only eleven men and a handful of women who followed Him after nearly four years of ministry.

Yes, the church has become deeply confused about its relationship with the state and its position and posture toward the issues of our day. The greatest loss in our generation is the perspective and purpose of a church that has come to the erroneous conclusion that a strong America is the same thing as a strong church; that a conservative victory on some level is equal to a Christian victory; that a moral culture is necessary for the church to have an impact.

Have we forgotten that our relationship to society is not to *reform* it, but to *redeem* it—one person at a time? Have we forgotten, in our power push for moral activism, that a man with good morals will die and go to hell as quickly as a man with bad morals?

This is spelled out clearly in the first two chapters of Romans where Paul delivers the surprising news that the man with proper morals (Romans 2) is as much on his way to hell as the man with perverted morals (Romans 1). That is why the church's mission is not to make bad people good, or good people better.

Our mission is not *moral* reformation, but *spiritual* reformation.

Politics can never achieve that end. The state does not have the equipment to bring about lasting change; only the gospel delivers a new nature. The courts simply do not have the tools to bring about spiritual change.

A classic case of this in the last hundred years was the church's role in prohibition. Many wonderful people, including women, pastors, and Christian leaders succeeded in influencing the outlawing of alcoholic beverages, only to create a wide opening for organized crime to fill the void and reap millions of dollars. Popular opinion eventually reneged and the church lost twice.

It may shock you, and it certainly would have the churches in the Prohibition Era, but the goal of the church was never to make drinking illegal. The mission, energy, and investment of the church was not then, and is not now, to clean up the evils of society; the mission of the church is to evangelize society.

Imagine if homosexuality was illegal; abortion was outlawed; sexual relations outside of marriage were unacceptable; prayer was back in the classroom, and the Ten Commandments were re-hung in the courtrooms. Would more people be going to heaven? Would the mission of the church be accomplished?

Suppose we could turn the clock back to the good old days with shared boundaries of morality; a basic respect for God; a common belief in absolute truth; an embarrassment over adultery; when sexual acts and aberrations were kept in the closet. Would we *then* breathe a sigh of relief?

Let's not stop there. What if we had our way in Washington, DC? What if evangelical counsel was the only counsel accepted; every piece of legislation we cared about passed in our favor? Would we wipe the sweat off our brow?

I believe the church today would, because the church at large has forgotten the nature of our battle. We are sweating over good *things*, but over the wrong *cause*. This does not mean that we do not care what society does! Given our current freedom, we vote against evil at every opportunity and rejoice when the court upholds moral purity. For those called into civil service, you should utilize that framework to shine as a light and influence those around you, just as a college student should seek to influence his roommates to avoid drugs.

In the meantime, the church could learn from farmers who realize that you can bring a pig inside your house, give him a bath and put a bow around his neck, and marvel at how good he smells. You can say, "There now, Mr. Pig, this is the right way to live." And Mr. Pig will grunt back in agreement. But the minute you take that pig out for a walk and pass a mud puddle, he is going to do a high dive right into the middle of it!

What happened? For starters, you cleaned the outside of the pig, but not the inside. You changed his environment, but not his nature. You brought him into your *home*, but you did not change his *heart*.

That is the problem with the distraction of the church today. It has bought the logic that if we can just keep sodomy illegal, we will have won a victory; but that depends on how you determine victory. Victory is not changing the behavior of our culture unless we have first changed its belief about who Jesus Christ is and how He alone transforms. Spiritual transformation does not happen from the outside in, but from the inside out.

The hope for Washington, DC—and our culture—is the same as that for the person who works in the cubicle next to you. It is Jesus Christ's saving gospel and a transformation of their heart by way of the cross. When people begin following Christ at His word, their voting decisions, moral parameters, vocabulary, and goals will be radically reversed by the renewing of their mind. Life will dramatically change as a result of the penetrating, life-changing Word of God. *That* is our mission.

The power of the Word of God and the mission of impacting people for Christ were the focus of the Apostle Paul's ministry. When he entered the Las Vegas of the ancient world, known as Corinth, it was a city so wicked and so decadent that if you wanted to say a woman was "loose," you would say she was a *Corinthian girl*. In fact, the church in Corinth would be composed of former embezzlers, homosexuals, adulterers, idolaters, and drunkards (1 Corinthians 6).

Yet, Paul never started a campaign to clean up the city's morals. He never organized voters to fill government positions with Christian-friendly officials. No doubt, Christians would speak their mind about pornography, prostitution, gambling, adultery, homosexuality, idolatry, and every other sin that plagued Corinth. However, their mission was not to clean up Corinth, but to deliver the gospel to people who would then become new creations in Christ.

Paul wrote to officials who served in Caesar's household, but he wrote not a word of undermining or influencing Caesar. He wrote not a whisper of conspiracy, unlike Dietrich Bonhoeffer who plotted with others to assassinate Adolph Hitler. Paul wrote not a word of secret meetings to overthrow Rome. Nothing in the inspired letters to the New Testament churches speaks about mounting a cultural war.

This was the error of Peter before the crucifixion. He determined that the current attitude toward Jesus Christ had reached a point of no return. They were about to arrest and lead away an innocent man—the God-man, no less. So Peter drew his sword! He said, in effect, "I will fight this cultural digression with the same weapons they are using against us. I'll match sword with sword; political muscle with muscle."

So Peter swung away, and an ear fell to the ground. Then, to the surprise of everyone, including His disciples, Jesus Christ reached out and healed the wounded man's ear—immediately relieving the pain of the one who had come to bring Him great pain. Jesus looked at Peter and said, "Have you forgotten that if I wanted to, I could call twelve legions of angels?" (Matthew 26) In other words, "Peter, if we wanted to fight them using their weapons, I could snap My finger and call to My side 72,000 angels."

So, if Peter's response was wrong, just how was the first-century believer to respond to Rome?

We must remember that when Paul wrote to the Roman believers there was no record of any Christian on the Roman senate. There was no Christian political lobby; no watchdog committee to make sure that the interests of the Christians were being addressed. There were no courts where false accusations against Christians could be resolved. In fact, when the barbarians sacked Rome, the Romans decided that it was the Christian's fault and persecution intensified. When Paul wrote the book of Romans, he made no reference, much less encouragement, to overthrow Nero. Instead, he wrote a text of Scripture that must have confounded them by its clear declarations.

TWO DECLARATIONS

Submission to government is the command of God.

> *Every person is to be in subjection to the governing authorities. 13:1a*

This is not a suggestion; this is a command. Other passages will deal with responding to government when they demand that we violate the clear command of God. Then we say, with the apostles who were told to stop spreading the gospel, that we will not obey!

The institution of government is the creation of God.

> *For there is no authority except from God,*
> *and those which exist are established by*
> *God. 13:1b*

One thing is certain; if Paul was talking about Nero, Rome, and his godless culture propped up by idolatrous leaders, what could that mean for us?

SIX OBSERVATIONS

The Christian is to obey the civil laws of government, *regardless* of that government's response to the gospel.

Wicked or righteous, the believer is not to make the promotion of, or the downfall of the government his mission.

A moral government or nation is *not* necessary to have a thriving church.

When Paul wrote his letter to the Romans, the culture was at its most depraved level. There were no sexual norms—heterosexuality was considered prudish; the emperor publicly married a *man;* pedophilia, adultery, and idolatry were rampant in Rome.

Yet, Christ determined that this was the Empire in which He would plant the living church—and the church would *thrive*!

It is not necessary for the church to have influence and freedom in order to be *faithful*.

In our generation, the church in China is surprising the free world with its rapid multiplication. Persecution seems to be acting as spiritual fertilizer, causing miraculous growth!

We are not commanded to battle cultural immorality or even expected to diminish it, but to *shine* **as light.**

Have you ever noticed that a lighthouse never once calmed a storm? It never redirected a hurricane. It never calmed the rolling ocean. The church is a lighthouse. Christians shine brightest when culture is darkest.

We have *never* **been told to depend upon God while pinning our hopes on reversing cultural trends.**

The moment we believe this, we will disband the purpose and mission of the church to make disciples. Our focus will turn to giving society a bath, trying to put a bow around its neck, and saying, "There, isn't that better?"

While the Ten Commandments are being taken down, many Christian leaders have refocused their energy on getting a secular courtroom to reverse their attitude. Let's face it, everyone in their right mind knows they should, simply because the laws of God form the very *basis* of our judicial system. However, the real issue is what caused our society to reach the point where the Ten Commandments were no longer wanted.

Well-meaning brothers and sisters in Christ are saying that we must keep the Ten Commandments in the courtrooms or all is lost in this culture war.

If there was ever a verse to restore the mission of the believer in our times, it comes from Paul's direction to Timothy, a young pastor trying to keep the church on course during a time when the church naturally wondered how it should live in the face of an ungodly world.

> *First of all, then, I urge that entreaties and prayers, petitions and thanksgivings, be made on behalf of all men, ²for kings and all who are in authority, so that **we may lead a tranquil and quiet life in all godliness and dignity.** ³This is good and acceptable in the sight of God our Savior. (1 Timothy 2:1–3)*

You will not find the slightest suggestion that we fight government with the same weapons they use; that we fight power with power; that we attempt to stem the tide of perversion with coalitions, boycotts, sit-ins, and marches. Our weapons are not the weapons of the world. We are not given a biblical mandate to wield political power and settle political appointments.

Go back in history to the time when Constantine made Christianity the religion of his culture; baptisms were politically correct; and allegiance to the church was expected. What was the result? The church became as corrupt as the world it tried to reach.

God has not called the church to replace, repair, or revive government. According to Romans 13, God has ordained the governments of this world for a purpose, and the church has been ordained for another purpose.

But take heart, according to Romans 13:1, God is sovereign over the governments of the world. Jesus Christ is in control of the nations of this world—*right now!*

Paul made this clear as he preached to the Athenian leaders in Acts 17:26.

> *He [God] made…every nation of mankind to live on all the face of the earth, having determined their appointed times and the boundaries of their habitation,*

It was God who had created their boundaries, their borders, their might, and the length of their existence as a nation.

This has not changed in the twenty-first century. God is not in heaven wringing His hands over the future of America. He is not breaking a sweat over the turmoil in the Middle East. He is not worried by the ever-present menace of Russia nor the growing antagonism of China. He is not wondering which country will do what, next. Neither is God hoping the Supreme Court in America will protect biblical morals and the freedoms of believers. *There has never been an emergency meeting of the Trinity!*

Have we forgotten that God is the sovereign ruler over the nations? God has never been elected, and He is not up for re-election any time soon!

We who are citizens of heaven belong to the royal family of the coming King. We should be model citizens of whatever country we belong to—praying for our leaders, acting as salt and light, shining in the darkness, and creating a thirst for God by our quiet dignity.

> *For our citizenship is in heaven*
> *(Philippians 3:20a)*

We ultimately pledge allegiance to heaven.

Does that mean we cannot pledge allegiance to our country? Certainly we can. In fact, while it remains a confession of the sovereignty of God, I recommend you pledge as often as you can. When you get to the part where it says, "one nation under God," talk louder! Just remember that your ultimate allegiance is to another country.

When Paul wrote to the Philippians that their citizenship was in heaven, he used the Greek word *politeuma* for citizenship, which is the word from which we get our word, "politics." Paul is effectively saying that our truest loyalty, our highest allegiance, is to heaven. We are to lobby heaven for God's cause on earth. We should recognize that our watchdog committees are in the heavens. We are to speak and act as ambassadors of our heavenly country. Paul reminded the Corinthians of this when he wrote,

> *Therefore, we are ambassadors for Christ*

And, the content of our diplomatic assignment is,

> *…we beg you on behalf of Christ, be reconciled to God. (2 Corinthians 5:20)*

Abraham Vema is a native of India and a Ph.D. graduate from Dallas Theological Seminary. He has designed a ministry of meeting with the top two hundred leaders of nations in our world. He offers counsel and spiritual guidance to the ambassadors of the United Nations. He has been granted by the Lord the gifts that allow him to stand before kings and princes. He is acting in that arena as light. He recently said to me, "If I can lead a nation's president to Christ, he will impact that nation for Christ. If I can win an ambassador to Christ, he will influence his arena for the gospel…that is ultimate victory."

Abraham's perspective would resonate with Paul, who encourages our purpose to be entirely redemptive. He takes the gospel to heads of state; to these men and women, knowing that if their hearts are changed by the Spirit of God, their way of thinking will be changed, their goals will be changed, their policies will be changed, and their countries can be influenced to change as well. It is change from the inside out!

It is time for the church to get back to the business of being the church. That does not mean a Christian cannot be involved in politics anymore than a Christian cannot be involved in building computers. If that is the arena God has called you into—like Daniel of old—raise your voice for the glory of God in that administration.

For Daniel, two kings bowed their heads to the glory of Israel's God; three administrations were deeply influenced by Daniel's character. He did not undermine Darius. He did not plot against Nebuchadnezzar. He did not raise up an army of Hebrews after Belshazzar's blasphemy against the sacred things of God. He shone! And God chose to bless Daniel's influence—which included being thrown into a pit of lions.

However, do not overlook the fact that at the time of Daniel's godly influence, God chose to bring an end to each kingdom and each administration—even *after* two of the kings trusted in the God of Daniel. In fact, an underlying message of Daniel's prophecy is that the kingdoms of this world will *all* pass away until we enter the kingdom of our Lord and Savior Jesus Christ.

Let us not forget our battle is not against flesh and blood, but against the rulers of darkness; our battle is not cultural, it is spiritual.

We have not been called by God to save America; we have been called by God to save *Americans*.

We have not been called by God to save America any more than Paul was to save Rome, or Martin Luther was to save Germany, or Charles Spurgeon was to save England.

America will one day fall—heaven will not. The city of man, Augustine reminded us, will one day be destroyed, but the city of God will last forever.

CONCLUSION

For the last 2,000 years, this has been the mission of the church—go into the city of man, through whatever avenue God has allowed you, and make disciples for the city of God. "Baptizing them and teaching them to obey what Jesus Christ commanded us to do" (Matthew 28:19–20 paraphrase). It is time for the church to become satisfied once again with obedience to our unique commission from God.

We have weapons the world does not have; we have power the governments of the world cannot imagine. We have power over death, the grave, and hell itself. We have One who is living within us who is greater than anyone that is in the world.

We are standing on the rock in the middle of a storm. So let us stop acting as if we are scrambling for a piece of driftwood in case the rock goes under.[1] The church of Jesus Christ is not sinking. Though Satan might try, the gates of hell will not prevail against it (Matthew 16:18).

We are ambassadors of the King sent to introduce our world to the true gospel. For the gospel is the power of God unto salvation to everyone who believes (Romans 1:16).

It is time for the church to get back to the business of being the church!

✝

Therefore whoever resists authority has opposed the ordinance of God; and they who have opposed will receive condemnation upon themselves.

[3]For rulers are not a cause of fear for good behavior, but for evil. Do you want to have no fear of authority? Do what is good and you will have praise from the same; [4]for it is a minister of God to you for good. But if you do what is evil, be afraid; for it does not bear the sword for nothing; for it is a minister of God, an avenger who brings wrath on the one who practices evil. [5]Therefore it is neccessary to be in subjection, not only because of wrath, but also for conscience' sake.

Chapter 2

Staying On Task

Romans 13:2–5

The Bible has a number of verses that are hard to understand—even harder to obey. One of them appears in Paul's exhortation that Timothy was to pursue a life of quiet dignity (2 Timothy 2:1, 2).

In light of the sin and chaos of his world, it would seem to have been the perfect time for Timothy to turn on a bullhorn, pick up a placard, sign a petition, and scorch society from the pulpit! Instead, the Apostle Paul commands the exact opposite response.

I am convinced that our problem is not that we do not *understand* this passage, but that we do not want to *obey* it. It certainly isn't easy to obey, any more than it is easy for a woman who is married to an unbelieving husband to win him *without a word* (1 Peter 3:1).

Not only is Peter's command difficult to obey, it appears that the logic is reversed. Does he really expect a Christian wife to win her unbelieving husband, not by putting tracts in his lunch bag or sermon cassettes in his car radio, but without a word?

For any woman married to an unbeliever to pursue his redemption by quiet character, a dramatic change in perspective will be required.

The church as well needs a dramatic alteration to its current pursuit of societal redemption. Here's what Paul had to say:

> *Every person is to be in subjection to the governing authorities. For there is no authority except from God, and those which exist are established by God.*
>
> *[2]Therefore whoever resists authority has opposed the ordinance of God; and they who have opposed will receive condemnation upon themselves.*
>
> *[3]For rulers are not a cause of fear for good behavior, but for evil. Do you want to have no fear of authority? Do what is good and*

you will have praise from the same; ⁴for it
is a minister of God to you for good. But if
you do what is evil, be afraid; for it does not
bear the sword for nothing; for it is a min-
ister of God, an avenger who brings wrath
on the one who practices evil. 13:1–4

THE BELIEVERS' RELATIONSHIP TO GOVERNMENT

In the previous chapter, we briefly identified six general principles of the believers' relationship to government. Let's examine four in greater detail.

The Christian is to obey every ordinance of government, in so far as it does not require him to abandon his conscience, his worship of God, or his obedience to Scripture.

This may not seem right to you. You might say, "Surely the believers in Rome would have every right in a decaying Roman culture, to violate the laws of that pagan state. Unquestionably the believer, who is now part of a new race and belonging to a new kingdom, can abandon the city of man and refuse to obey or even participate in his culture."

However, the Bible says exactly the opposite—later in Romans 13, Paul will clearly tell the believer to pay his taxes, provide honor where it is due, and follow the customs of the land, in so far as they do not demand a violation of God's commands.

Daniel is a classic example of a believer's right relationship to government. He was taken to a foreign land and immediately required to eat the king's meat and drink the king's wine. Since the king's meat would have included unclean animals that were forbidden by God and the king's wine would have been previously offered as a libation to the gods, Daniel asked permission to eat vegetables and drink water. Though Daniel would not participate in an activity that defied God's laws, he was obedient in every other area. One such area was the changing of his name, for it was changed from Daniel to Belteshazzar. This was part of the psychological deprogramming that Nebuchadnezzar had strategically planned to turn these sharp Jewish lads into Babylonians. One of his plans was to eliminate the constant reminder of the theological truths embedded in their names by replacing them with pagan names. *Daniel* means, "God is my Judge or Ruler." *Belteshazzar* means, "Baal's prince." In the past, every time his name had been called, Daniel was reminded that "God was Ruler." Now, every time he would be called or referenced, he would be called the "prince of Baal." Daniel never refused that pagan name. Why? No just law of God had been violated.

As Paul commanded, and as Daniel practiced, we too must obey the laws of government, even when we don't like them. For instance, the church I pastor must obey the ordinances of the city no matter how expensive and frustrating. If we build a new auditorium, the city will tell us how many seats it can have, based on how many parking spaces are outside. They will tell us how many exit doors we must build, how many sprinkler systems we must install, and how many fire alarms we must include. They have regulated a hundred different things on our current buildings, including how tall and how wide the church sign could be.

What right does the city have to tell the church of the living God how tall our sign can be? To this day people do not even see our sign. They think we are a college or a government building. We have people in our church who had driven by our site for years unaware that we were a church. Our church sign is nearly worthless. Why not fight it? Since the city is not asking us to violate God's commands by putting up a small sign, we must obey every ordinance no matter how ridiculous.

**A moral government is not necessary for
the church to fulfill its mission.**

If a moral government was necessary, then the apostles would have clearly instructed the church on the importance of solidifying a Christian voting bloc to bring moral parameters to bear in society or stated the necessity of moral public officials, rulers, and magistrates in order for the church to be successful. Instead, we discover the opposite challenge.

Erwin Lutzer correctly identifies the urgent need in our culture.

> Our nation needs an antidote that is far more radical than politics could ever be. Our so-called culture war is really a spiritual war. Our problems are not fundamentally abortion, trash television, and homosexual values. The root of our cultural decay is first and foremost spiritual; we must attack the root of this corrupt tree. Our greatest challenge is theological, not political and cultural.[2]

**The mission of the church is not moral
reformation, but spiritual transformation.**

Since a moral government is not necessary for a thriving church, then it is illogical and unproductive for the church to focus on moral reformation. Over the last twenty-five years of ecclesiastical activism, we have forgotten the mission of the believer and the church. It is not the business of the Christian to keep his culture from plunging into wickedness. *Our mission is not to make bad people good.*

Have we forgotten that good people are not *going* to be condemned by God, but are condemned *already* (John 3:18)?

Have we forgotten that a policeman can go to hell as quickly as a prostitute; that an upstanding judge is as guilty before God as the criminals he sends to jail? That is why, as Kevin Bauder clearly articulates,

> The church as a whole, and Christians as individuals were never given the charge from God to halt or even diminish the evil practices in their societies.[3]

Does this mean we do not care? Of course not! However, it does mean we pursue change in our society one disciple at a time.

It sounds old fashioned to suggest that the mission of the church in impacting society is to act like salt and light, so that the world might see our good works and glorify God. However, that is our mission! Our mission is spiritual reformation. We strike at the root of the problem, not at its symptoms.

Even in the Old Testament, the illustrations of God's messengers remain the same. Jonah was never told to go to Nineveh and influence the king away from idolatry. He was never told to lobby to have child sacrifices outlawed. He was never told to go and reform Nineveh.

Jonah went to Nineveh as God's messenger with the same message that we have for our world and that Paul had for his world, "Repent…God is angry with your wickedness! Don't forget, it is appointed unto man once to die and after that the judgment…"

What did Nineveh do? They repented! They fell on their faces before the message of this God of justice and patience, who would give them time to repent. Guess what happened to child sacrifice? It stopped! Guess what happened to idolatry? It ceased!

If we shift our focus to the ministry of Jesus Christ, we notice that He was more concerned with the corruption among the so-called people of God than with the governments and civil systems of His day.

One author's assessment of Christ's ministry demands contemplation.

Jesus Christ never made calls for political or social reform, even by peaceful means. He never at-

tempted to capture the culture for biblical morality or to gain greater freedom [for His followers].
He did not come to proclaim or establish a new
social or moral order but a new spiritual order;
His church. He did not seek to make the old creation moral, but to make His new creations holy.
There was no effort on His part to eliminate social or political injustice, [although His followers
would live such lives of purity and integrity and
compassion, that social structures would be af-
fected for the next 2,000 years].[4]

The most powerful tools of God on planet earth are
not moral governments but godly believers and pure
churches. The first are nice, but the second are necessary.

Our true battle is not against corrupt government but
against the kingdom of darkness. The kingdom which has
blinded the minds of the world to believe that God is not
watching; that God is not even around. This is the reason
our real battle is spiritual.

To attempt to vote through, push through, influence,
cajole, petition, and march to see moral advancement is to
miss the mark as the church.

Erwin Lutzer illustrated it in this way,

We can argue with our culture that Christian
morality is better; we can move to clean up our

culture by legislation and boycotts. But our efforts will be like trying to mop up the floor with the faucet running. Because we are trying to convince citizens of earth to live as though they are citizens of heaven and they are not buying it.[5]

This is not the first time in world history that the church has had the responsibility of representing Christ when society as a whole has abandoned God. And when this has happened, the most effective ministry occurred when the church realized it was not an agent of moral confrontation but an agent of spiritual reformation.[6]

Becoming co-belligerents, as Francis Schaeffer defined it, has never resulted in a spiritual reformation. Joining other Christians to take back lost ground in the social and political arena has only caused the testimony of Christ to suffer and compromised the theology and mission of the church.

There are well-meaning people who are preaching that we must reclaim America for Christ. I know it sounds exciting, and it is the easier message to preach on Sunday mornings, but it presupposes several wrong things.

It implies that Jesus Christ had America at one point, but lost it. It also implies that America was once thoroughly Christian, when neither it nor any other nation ever was. It also presupposes that Jesus Christ now wants America back and implies that for Him to get America back we have to get the leaders and citizens of America to behave, whether they believe in Jesus Christ or not. What kind of message is that? It is not the message of Jesus Christ.

Study the preaching and theology of Christ, and you'll discover He never intended for His disciples to claim or reclaim nations, but to go into all the nations and preach the gospel to kingdoms that were passing away—whose boundaries and times of existence were already determined by a sovereign Lord (Acts 17:26).

It might tickle our patriotic ears to hear a call to win America back. However, according to Scripture, our mission is not to win America, but to win Americans to Christ.

Our mandate on earth is not to save our nation, but to bring individuals from this and every nation to salvation by faith in Jesus Christ alone.

Since our goal is spiritual reformation, it extends well beyond our borders. Our mission is wrapped up in our charge—the proclamation of the gospel. That is life-changing—society-changing—world-changing power. It is,

> ...the power of God through salvation...
> (Romans 1:16)

To swap our gospel for political activism, which hopes the government will become the *ally* of the church and adopt the morals of the Christian, is to imply that the gospel is not powerful enough, fast enough, or good enough. More importantly, it *neglects* our mission and ultimately *distorts* our gospel.

It is the spiritual equivalent of a heart surgeon abandoning his profession to become a make-up artist, spending his time making people look better rather than saving lives. The mission of the church is not to change our nation—although it may be the by-product of believers who live faithful lives of ministry and purity—but the mission of Christianity is to join the Father who seeks those who will worship Him in spirit and in truth.

Do you understand what this implies?

This means that legislation regarding the rights of homosexuals is not our mission; the eternal destiny of homosexuals is. The success or failure of legislation regarding abortion is not nearly as significant as the souls of women who are struggling with the guilt of having their unborn killed. Whether or not prayer returns to the classroom is not the issue for Christians to sign petitions and deluge Washington with e-mails; being heard as the voice that explains who God is, and how He must be approached through prayer, *is* the issue.

In fact, if prayer returned to the public school system today, then prayer on Monday might be to the Jewish God; prayer on Tuesday to Jesus Christ; prayer on Wednesday to Allah; prayer on Thursday to Krishna; and prayer on Friday to a universal power.

We must understand that what the courts decide on euthanasia or evolution, what will be taught in the public arena, and what will be allowed in the medical laboratories is not nearly as critical as the eternal destiny of human beings.

> We have a message that only we can deliver…it must be heard above the din of political posturing and power. We have an agenda that is divinely inspired…it is more important than saving America; it is holding the cross of Jesus Christ high so that God might be pleased to save Americans.[7]

To save some by the gospel was the passion of Paul. This must be our passion for we are in a lifeboat on the sea of human history, surrounded at this very moment by people who are dying. We dare not become distracted in our mission as churches or as individuals. We do not throw the drowning masses books on how to tread water longer; we do not attempt to make the water more comfortable; we do not sell them better swim suits; we do not exhort them to try the backstroke; our message is clear—the kingdom of this world is passing away. Their sin has placed them in grave danger for the Creator of the ocean has designed it so that they will not be able to avoid eternal judgment on their own. Their only hope is Jesus Christ.

You may remember E. V. Hill, the pastor of Mount Zion Missionary Baptist Church in Los Angeles. I was reading the fascinating book *Two Cities, Two Loves*, which is James Montgomery Boice's exposition on the subject of the Christian and politics. Boice mentioned the story of Hill, who once served as a ward leader for the Democratic party.

Hill's assignment was to get out the vote for the Democratic candidates, and his chief strategy for doing this was to have a block captain for each block of his ward. On election day, the block captains were to contact each resident of their block to make sure they voted. When Hill came to Los Angeles and began pastoring the church, he was convicted by the thought that if he did this for the Democratic party, why shouldn't he do it for God; why not have a Christian block captain for every block of Los Angeles? It was not as absurd as it sounded.

In E. V. Hill's area of the city, south central Los Angeles, the number of city blocks was 3,100. That became the mission of this church. Boice said that when he first heard E. V. talk about this goal, they had already established a Christian presence in 1,900 blocks of their area. In fact, people were moving into a block for this very purpose. The church adopted an attitude that they existed for the sake of the gospel.

Hill tells of a funny thing that happened on one occasion. One man had been very put off by the block captain where he lived. She was always inviting him to services and other meetings of the church—always friendly, but persistent. He decided to move. In fact, he decided to move to the other side of Los Angeles. The truck came, and he loaded up his possessions. His block captain came out to say goodbye. The truck started off, and as soon as he was gone, the block captain went back into her house, got out the directory of the Mount Zion block captains, found the person in charge of the block to which her offended neighbor was moving, and when he turned onto his new street, there was the new block captain standing on the street in front of his new home to welcome him and invite him to church. His comment was classic, "My God, they're *everywhere*."[8]

That story is deeply convicting. What could we do if every Christian truly believed that they were called to their specific city, at this specific time, in this specific generation to deliver to every person the gospel of Jesus Christ?

Perhaps part of our problem is the same as E. V. Hill's was at one point, he had a greater passion for getting out the vote than he had for Jesus Christ.

Do not misunderstand, we should vote. I believe with Daniel Webster that, "Whatever makes good Christians, makes them good citizens."

But if our passion and energy and focus is on getting out the vote, then our passion is for the temporal, transient governments of our world while our eternal mission stands neglected.[9] While we are occupied with good things, we are missing eternal things.

BELIEVERS' RESPONSIBILITY TO GOVERNMENT

Returning our attention to Romans 13, we are reminded of the shocking news Paul delivers to the Roman believers concerning the obligation of the believer to governmental authority.

Submission to government is the command of God.

> *Every person is to be in subjection to the governing authorities. 13:1*

The word *subjection* is a military term which means, "to fall under the rank of another." This word refers to obeying the commands of government as a junior officer obeys a superior officer. When a superior officer orders a new recruit to, "Give me forty, right now," the soldier does not say, "But, why?" or "I don't feel like it." He just drops to the ground and does forty push-ups.

This is simply an issue of authority, not a statement of value. The new soldier might be better, more honest, more upstanding, and more committed to the army than his commanding officer. It does not matter; he responds to authority with obedience.

When your authority, the one dressed not in army green, but gray or blue, pulls up behind you with flashing lights, how do you respond? I don't know about you, but I automatically say, "Yes, sir."

I was driving home after spending time with my wife and two daughters at the state fair. We were talking, laughing, and absolutely exhausted. My good mood was attributed not only to their presence but also to having eaten that North Carolina State Fair specialty—deep-fried Oreos. Life was good!

Suddenly, there were flashing lights behind me. I was not speeding and did not know what I had done, but I would soon find out. Evidently, when I had turned right, I rolled through the stop sign and had crossed the yellow dividing line. I'm not sure the officer understood how hard it is to turn sharply when you have just eaten deep-fried Oreos, but did I argue with him? Absolutely not! He is my authority. He asked to see my driver's license, and I promptly replied, "Yes, sir...sir...here you are, sir!"

For the believer, responding to civil authorities with respect and obedience unless commanded to violate godly conscience or biblical commands, *is* the command of God.

The institution of government is the creation of God.

While the first part of Romans 13:1 has to do with the *obligation* of the believer to government, the next portion of the verse reminds the believer of the *origin* of government.

> *For there is no authority except from God, and those which exist are established by God. 13:1b*

You might have noticed that the word *authority* appears many times in this chapter. It has already appeared twice in verse 1.

In the original language, there are two words used for political power that are altogether different. The word *kratos* refers to "rule" or "the power of ruling." It is used of someone who has the power to decide. This word *kratos*, which means "power," when combined with the word *demos*, which means "people," forms *demokratos*, or *democracy*. This has the meaning, "the power of people," or "rule by the people."

The other word that is used for political power is *exousia*, which means, "delegated power." It is power granted by someone more powerful to one less powerful to act on his behalf. This is the word that is used four times by Paul in Romans chapter 13.

The authority of the government is delegated power from God. If God did not give power to both godly and ungodly governments of the world, they would never rise to power. It is *from* God that these powers have come, and it is *to* God that these powers are accountable. So here in one word, is both the legitimacy and accountability of human government.[10]

Jesus' acknowledged the divine source of governmental power when He stood before Pontius Pilate, accused of treason. During the interrogation, Pilate kept asking Jesus questions, but the Lord refused to answer. Finally, Pilate responded in frustration,

> *You do not speak to me? Do You not know that I have authority to release You, and I have authority to crucify You? (John 19:10)*

Observe the greatness of Jesus' response and imagine how encouraging this text would be to the persecuted church for the next 2,000 years.

> *You would have no authority over Me, unless it had been given you from above. (John 19:11a)*

49

That is the same word *exousia* that Paul used in Romans 13. In other words, "Pilate, the power you have to rule, and even to deliver Me over to be crucified, is power from on high. It is delegated authority."

> *For this reason he who delivered Me to you*
> *has the greater sin. (John 19:11b)*

"Pilate, you're going to stand accountable one day for your political decision to deliver Me up, but in the meantime, your decision happens to be the will of heaven."

What is the authority of government? Is it in the policeman's badge? Is it in the robe of the judge? Is it in the king's crown? No. Behind these symbols is the authority of God, for within every agency of law and civil authority is a sense of divine investment.[11]

Perhaps this is the reason that corrupt judges, cruel governments, and crooked officials are especially abhorrent to God. They are violating their ordained purpose from God, and they will stand accountable to Him one day!

Disobedience to government receives consequences from God.

Since government receives its authority from God, as it relates to submission to just law, the believer has no right to oppose or disobey.

> *Therefore whoever resists authority has op-*
> *posed the ordinance of God; and they who*
> *have opposed will receive condemnation*
> *upon themselves. 13:2*

In other words, opposition to government is opposition to God. The word *condemnation* could be rendered,
"judgment."[12]

When the believer disobeys government, he receives
two sets of discipline; one from the government for having
violated the law and the other from the Lord for having
violated His command.

> *Submit yourselves for the Lord's sake to ev-*
> *ery human institution, whether to a king*
> *as the one in authority, [14]or to governors as*
> *sent by Him for the punishment of evildo-*
> *ers and the praise of those who do right.*
> *[15]For such is the will of God...[17]honor all*
> *people; love the brotherhood, fear God,*
> *honor the king. (1 Peter 2:13–17)*

One might think, "Peter, you've got to be kidding! Do
you know who the king is? How can you tell us to honor
the Emperor? How do you honor Nero?" You honor the
Emperor by recognizing there is a higher, greater, eternal,
divine King, who holds the earthly Emperor in His hand.

The justice of government reveals the character of God.

> *For rulers are not a cause of fear for good*
> *behavior, but for evil. Do you want to have*
> *no fear of authority? Do what is good, and*
> *you will have praise from the same; [4]for*
> *it is a minister of God…an avenger who*
> *brings wrath on the one who practices evil.*
> *13:3–4*

Notice the contrast between good and evil. Even when government refuses to acknowledge God, they unintentionally represent the character of God by punishing evil and rewarding good.

The word *avenger* is a word which means, "to exact a penalty." The government has established penalties for doing wrong; that is God's purpose for government. Even the unbeliever who says he does not believe in absolute moral truth inherently knows right from wrong.

Experiment with your atheist neighbor sometime by driving his car without permission. Drive over the bushes he just planted between your yard and his and then back into his mailbox and knock it over.

"Hey," he will say, "you can't do that!"

"Why not?"

"Because it's against the law. The law says you can't do those mean things to me!"

"Who said they're mean? They don't bother me!"

Your experiment will surely reveal that even your atheist neighbor believes in moral law.

The only valid basis for moral law is a previously existing morality. No matter where you go in the world, stealing or damaging your neighbor's possessions is considered *wrong*.

God ordained government to reflect His moral law: His attributes of justice, equity, impartiality, righteousness, and honesty. That means government must be concerned with moral issues because laws are based on the moral perfection of God.

However, this is not the same as saying the government can develop morality in its citizens. It can prescribe penalties. It can enforce them and perhaps, restrain evil. But it cannot change the people involved.[13]

The only thing that changes people is the power of God working through the gospel. The solution for an immoral society is not more law. Mankind has already developed thousands of laws to try and uphold ten commandments. No, the solution is not more government—it is the gospel.

I PLEDGE ALLEGIANCE

APPLICATION

Let me close this chapter with two encouragements to stay on task.

Remember your mission!

We are to go and make what? Disciples! Followers of Jesus Christ! Learners of the Savior! God has not called us to go and make bad people better. He has not called us to go and make moral people. He has not commissioned us to go and make monotheists, for even monotheists can die and go to hell.

> *You believe that God is one. You do well;*
> *the demons also believe, and shudder.*
> *(James 2:19)*

The mission of the church is not even to go and make converts; our mission is to go and make disciples.

A disciple influences his world, whether he or she is a lawyer, a politician, a member of the PTA, a computer salesman, a mechanic, a doctor, or a housewife. For all of us, our mission is the same; the only difference is our sphere of influence.

Cal Thomas was one of the architects of the failed Moral Majority of the 1980's. The methods of the organi-

54

zation have been picked up by The Christian Coalition and in more recent years by Focus on the Family. Cal Thomas has since moved on to enter the world of journalism. He wrote a fascinating book entitled *Blinded By Might* that chronicles the flawed reasoning of Christian involvement in political activism. In an article published in *Newsweek* a few years ago, he wrote, "For Christians, the vision of worldly power [and influence] is not a calling, but a distraction. It is a temptation that Jesus Christ Himself rejected, not because it was dangerous, but because it was trivial, compared with His mission."[14]

Let us remember the mission He gave His disciples before leaving this earth,

> *Go and make disciples of all the nations, baptizing them and* [20]*teaching them to [obey] all that I commanded you. (Matthew 28:19–20)*

Reaffirm your message!

You are a chosen race, a royal priesthood… that you may proclaim the excellencies of Him who has called you out of darkness into His marvelous light. (1 Peter 2:9)

We proclaim eternal life. (1 John 1:2)

How many politicians have heard from Christians regarding their views, their disappointments, their frustrations, even their threats? Yet, how many hear the gospel?

One author was interviewed by a reporter who was covering Christian leaders and their opinions on various issues. At the end of their interview, this author asked the reporter, "Has anyone shared with you the gospel?" The reporter asked with total innocence and honesty, "What is the gospel?" While this reporter knew where Christians stood on the issues, sadly she had no idea of the Christian message of faith in Christ.

C. S. Lewis has become a household name among our world of unbelievers with the release of a movie based on his book series, *The Chronicles of Narnia*. This brilliant Christian author has impacted millions of people with the truth of the gospel in his writings.

C. S. Lewis spoke insightfully and almost prophetically to our day.

> "If you read history you will find that the Christians who did most for the present world were just those who thought the most of the next…It is since Christians have largely ceased to think of the other world that they have become so ineffective in this world. Aim at heaven and you will get earth 'thrown in.' Aim at earth and you will get neither. In the same

way we shall never save civilisation [*sic*] as long as civilisation [*sic*] is our main object. We must learn to want something else even more."[15]

Let us stay on task. Let us remember our mission. Let us reaffirm our message. Let us return to our gospel focus that makes the church great and brings honor and dignity to the cause of Jesus Christ.

✝

For because of this you also pay taxes, for rulers are servants of God, devoting themselves to this very thing. [7]Render to all what is due them: tax to whom tax is due; custom to whom custom; fear to whom fear; honor to whom honor.

Chapter 3

Paying Your Dues

Romans 13:6–7

Open a newspaper on any given day and you will read yet another story that reveals the downward plunge of our culture into greater sin and bolder defiance of God's standard. Without a doubt, believers could grow frustrated, worried, even angry!

We have watched over the years as:

- Public courts have sanctioned as alternate lifestyle what we know to be sinful homosexual behavior, and liberal churches and seminaries are carrying that torch today.

- A public uproar arose over the suggestion of the Pope that homosexual men not be allowed to enter

Catholic seminaries, which is hard to imagine, given the multiple tens of millions of dollars the Catholic church has lost because of pervasive pedophilia within the priesthood.

- Reproductive freedom—which interpreted means a woman's right to have an abortion granting freedom for her, but death for her baby—has become the accepted viewpoint not only of the courts of our land, but of thousands of people in our country who claim to be Christians.

- The average school and government agency has promoted the practice of safe sex, as if sexual activity outside of marriage can ever be considered *safe*, while sexual promiscuity and its resulting diseases have reached epidemic proportions.

- "Freedom of speech" has been used to defend pornographic literature, film, and art exhibitions in which Jesus Christ is depicted as blasphemously as the artist chooses, while any true depiction of Christ has become unacceptable.

It is certainly understandable for believers to be troubled. We are watching Romans chapter 1 unfold in our nation, much like the first-century believer saw the collapse of moral structure in Rome.

Our society is on a trajectory toward destruction, and our only hope is the only hope any society has ever had— the gospel. What is alarming is that we happen to be the generation that is experiencing the transition from a society that upheld many of our biblical values to a pluralistic society that believes truth is no longer absolute.

The church, in the last twenty and thirty years, has responded to this transition in a variety of ways. One of the most popular ways, cycling through a variety of name changes and leaders, is Christian political activism.

During the past few decades, well-meaning Christians have organized powerful coalitions, activist organizations, and political muscle machines to combat the digression of evil in our American culture. Two individuals deeply involved in the process admitted to making no ground. Now, years later, listen to these men who gave their lives to Christian political activism.

- Gary Bauer, former president of the Family Research Council, an offshoot of Focus on the Family, who eventually ran under the Christian banner for President, said, "There is virtually *nothing* to show for an 18-year commitment."[16]

- Cal Thomas was a key architect in building Jerry Falwell's activist movement in the 1980's, known as the Moral Majority. The Moral Majority was credited by even the secular media, as the coalition which brought Ronald Reagan to the presidency and a conservative majority to the Senate. Cal Thomas wrote about their election and their incredible sense of victory. They firmly believed they now had the necessary power to halt America's moral landslide. Thomas said this a few years ago, "Two decades after conservative Christians charged into the political arena, bringing new voters and millions of dollars with them in hopes of transforming the culture through political power, it must now be acknowledged that [it] *failed*."[17]

It *seemed* that progress was being made. Battles were won on the political front; pro-life candidates were elected. Surely the evil slide of our culture would be stopped, or at least, slowed down.

It never happened. Now, in the twenty-first century, well-meaning Christians are trying again with the same tactic, the same passion, the same strategy to stop the ever-increasing slide of society into sin.

This situation reminds me of what Robert Perry faced on one of his many polar expeditions, as he headed north with one of his dogsled teams. At the end of the day, when he stopped to take a bearing on his latitude, he was amazed to discover that he was actually further south than he had been at the beginning of the day—even though he had been hustling north all day long with his dogsled. The mystery was eventually solved when he discovered that he had been traveling on a gigantic ice floe. Ocean currents were pulling him south *faster* than the dog team could travel north.[18]

The ice floe is a great picture of our culture. No wonder Bauer and Thomas, now twenty-five years later, say we are further south than when we started. While the entire time, we *thought* we were moving north.

After two decades of involvement and millions of dollars and man hours, sin is more predominant than ever. Homosexuality is viewed as acceptable; in fact, we now have openly homosexual leaders. Sin is more openly embraced than ever before and, in the meantime, the church has developed a reputation of being only one more political voting bloc to contend with on election day. In the eyes of the world, we are clamoring for the same power, the same podium, the same position as them.

May I remind you that God is actually in control of the ice floe! He has set it on its course. This country and every country that has ever existed and will ever exist is under the pleasure, purpose, and power of God.

> *This is what the Lord Almighty, the God of Israel, says,* [5]*"Tell this to your masters; with My great power and outstretched arm*

I made the earth and its people and the
animals that are on it, and I will give it to
anyone I please."

⁶I will hand all your countries over to My
servant Nebuchadnezzar king of Babylon.
(Jeremiah 27:4–6a NIV)

Imagine Jeremiah's response to this revelation, "Wait a minute! You mean pagan, idolatrous, wicked, ruthless Nebuchadnezzar—he's Your candidate? Wait! Did I hear You call him, Your 'servant'?"

It is a flawed belief that because America began with the acknowledgement of a Creator and a respect for the Bible, it is somehow guaranteed favored status with God. It is equally flawed to believe that to protect America is paramount to protecting God; to defend America is the same as defending Christ's cause. And the belief that to keep America from embracing secularism, humanism, and liberalism is God's plan. This view binds the hope of the Christian to a voting booth.

Should we vote? Yes! In fact, not to do so would be to display a lack of gratitude for whatever amount of religious freedom and moral boundary our government yet endorses.

Remember, however, that Jesus Christ did not say, "I will build My *country*," even though I love my country. He did not say, "I will build this nation," even though I am extremely grateful for this nation. No, Jesus Christ said,

> *I will build My church; and the gates of Hades will not overcome it. (Matthew 16:18b)*

Does this mean we do not speak out against the evils of our society and government? Certainly not. We stand like John the Baptist who pointed his finger at Herod and called him an adulterer for marrying his sister-in-law.

> *[Herod] was afraid of John, knowing that he was a righteous and holy man. (Mark 6:20a)*

The Scottish reformer John Knox exemplified the attitude of John the Baptist when he called Bloody Mary a sinner and challenged her sinful ways. Queen Mary once said that she did not fear the armies of any empire, but she feared the *prayers* of John Knox.

The political leaders of our day may fear Christian pastors and ministry leaders, but not because we are righteous or because we are willing to speak the truth regardless of political correctness in our culture or our congregation. Christian leaders today are not feared for their prayers, they are feared because they have an ability to deliver the votes.[19]

Voting power has replaced preaching power and praying power. As a result, what the church is saying and what our world is hearing, is the message that prayer is not effective enough, the gospel is not powerful enough, discipleship is not fast enough—it might have been God's idea in the first century, but it is out of date in the twenty-first century.

Do we not care that our world is on an ice floe destined for destruction? Yes, we care! Therefore the ultimate issue will never be whether you are pro-life or pro-choice; pro-gay or anti-gay; pro-gun or anti-gun; pro-military or anti-military; Democrat, Republican, or Independent; pro-recycling or just put it all in one trash bag.

The ultimate issue is whether a person hears, understands, and accepts the primary message that only the Christian can deliver—the liberating, life-changing, redeeming gospel of Jesus Christ.

HOW DO CHRISTIANS RESPOND TO GOVERNMENT?

Submit

Since government is ordained by God and disobedience is punished by God, we are to submit to the governing authority.

Paul tells us the reason why.

> *Every person is to be in subjection to the governing authorities. For there is no authority except from God, and those which exist are established by God.*
>
> *²Therefore whoever resists authority has opposed the ordinance of God; and they who have opposed will receive condemnation upon themselves.*
>
> *³For rulers are not a cause of fear for good behavior, but for evil. Do you want to have no fear of authority? Do what is good and you will have praise from the same;*
>
> *⁴for it is a minister of God to you for good. But if you do what is evil, be afraid; for it does not bear the sword for nothing; for it is a minister of God, an avenger who brings wrath on the one who practices evil.*
>
> *⁵Therefore it is necessary to be in subjection, not only because of wrath, but also for conscience' sake. 13:1–5*

From these verses, we can easily summarize that the role of government is three-fold.

1. First, the government is to discourage evil.

    For rulers are not a cause of fear for good
    behavior, but for evil. 13:3a

    This Greek word for *fear* gives us the English word
    "phobia." In other words, the government creates a
    sense of phobia—all sorts of fears in the lives of those
    who commit evil deeds.

    This is only further proof that even ungodly, worldly
    rulers have a basic awareness of good and evil. To hin-
    der the digression of any culture into total anarchy,
    God has established government.[20]

2. Second, the government is to encourage good.

    Do what is good and you will have praise
    from the same; 13:3b

    In other words, obey the laws of the land, and as a gen-
    eral rule, you will be appreciated as a good citizen.

3. Third, the government is the minister of God to
    enforce punishment.

    For it does not bear the sword for nothing;
    for it is a minister of God, an avenger who
    brings wrath on the one who practices evil.
    13:4

The sword is a reference to the weapon used to maim and kill. Paul says it is the symbol of the government's right to punish crime, even with the penalty of death. God instituted the death penalty early in human history.

> *Whoever sheds man's blood, by man his blood shall be shed, for in the image of God He made man. (Genesis 9:6)*

The Apostle Paul further legitimized capital punishment when he appealed to speak before Caesar in the Roman court.

> *If, then, I am a wrongdoer and have committed anything worthy of death, I do not refuse to die. (Acts 25:11)*

In other words, it is right to have my life taken in judgment if I am guilty of crimes punishable by death.[21]

Maybe you think mankind is not really that bad and government should not have that kind of role. A role which can, and certainly has been misused over the course of human history. But it remains God's instrument, and the general rule is that the governing of mankind hinders evil, encourages good, and punishes evil.

Robert Haldane wrote over a century ago,

> The world, ever since the fall, has been in such a state of corruption and depravity, that without the powerful obstacle presented by civil government to the selfish and malignant passions of men, it would be better to live among the beasts of the forest than in human society. As soon as its restraints are removed, man shows himself in his real character.[22]

His observation is demonstrated daily. Look at the riots of Paris, France in November 2005. Read the reports of rape, theft, and murder in the streets of New Orleans following the flood waters of Hurricane Katrina. Turn off the lights in some major city for just one hour and watch humanity—free from the fear of accountability or justice—reveal its utter depravity and live as beasts.

When is it right to disobey government?

Maybe you are wondering if it is ever right to disobey the government. When the government demands that we *do* something that God says we should not do, or when the government demands that we *not do* something that God tells us to do, we must disobey.

Three examples recorded in the Bible demonstrate this.

1. The first one is regarding the protection of human life. The Hebrew midwives were commanded to kill the Hebrew baby boys and they refused. (Exodus 1)

2. The second one is regarding the issue of worshipping false gods. (Daniel 3)

3. The third case study is regarding the proclamation of the gospel and civil authorities demanding that Christians no longer evangelize. (Acts 5)

Other than in these instances, the Christian is to submit to the governing authorities.

Support

If you thought submitting to government was hard to swallow, try Paul's second command, which is to support the government.

> *For because of this you also pay taxes, for rulers are servants of God, devoting themselves to this very thing. 13:6*

Perhaps one of your favorite indoor sports is beating the government out of what is due. You may think, "They'll never spot that! There's no record of that income! They'll never be able to disprove that expense! Those crooked tax-collectors!"

You may think high taxes are a new problem, but the tax system of Paul's democratic society was certainly frustrating to the first-century believer. In its final years, the Roman Empire deteriorated into a huge welfare state in which the working class supported more and more people who did not work. It was also not unusual for Roman officials to use tax revenue to support pagan religious activities throughout the empire.[23]

Without a doubt, the Christians living in Rome wanted to know the answer to this question, "Since we are now citizens of another country, and our citizenship is in heaven, and our allegiance is ultimately to God, do we have to pay taxes?"

Paul answers:

> *Render to all what is due them: tax to whom tax is due. 13:7a*

The word Paul used in this verse for *tax* settled the question. It is the word *phoros* and it referred to tax on houses, land, property, and even income tax.[24] This word covered the gamut. In fact, the context indicates that Paul is referring to any and every kind of tax levied by the government.

For us today, this would include sales tax, utility tax, property tax, capital gains tax, inheritance tax, tax on perishables, automobiles, clothing, etc., etc., etc. You know the old saying, "There are two certainties in life—death and taxes." To which someone added, "I just wish they came in that order!"[25] They don't however, and we are commanded to pay all that we owe.

Within legal allowances, you may arrange your finances in such a way that you limit the amount of taxes you pay. So far, our country actually allows us to deduct from our taxes any and all charitable giving. Paul knew nothing of that. Still, the average person wants to get out of paying taxes entirely. According to a 2005 IRS Oversight Board Special Report, the percentage of Americans who now actually approve of cheating on their income taxes is 19%! The troubling thing about this statistic is not that one out of five Americans cheat on their taxes, or that one out of five admit it, but that one out of five has reached the point in his thinking that it is actually the right thing to do. They think breaking the law, in this instance, is not only acceptable, it is *advisable*.

Jim George, a Christian leader and writer, wrote a magazine article not long ago in which he told the story of trying to sell a used boat trailer in the middle of the winter.

It was below freezing outside and no one was interested in boating. Then a potential buyer contacted him and said he was willing to pay the full asking price! But there was one catch. He wanted Jim to put only half the price of the trailer on the bill of sale. That way, the buyer would only have to pay half the state sales tax, which would save him hundreds of dollars. The buyer said, "You know, that's the way we do it around here."

Jim wrote, "I really wanted to sell that trailer, and if I said no, he might back out. If I agreed, I'd be lying, breaking the law, but who would know? I knew what I should do, but I was having this inner struggle. Finally, I told him I was a Christian and couldn't do anything illegal. The man went ahead and bought the trailer anyway, and I declared the full amount on the bill of sale."[26]

Unlike Jim, many Americans, even some believers, cheat on their taxes. I have read that the amount of income taxes *never* paid to the government comes to more than ninety-three billion dollars a year! Is some of that *your* money?

But Paul does not stop with taxes.

> *Render to all what is due them: custom to whom custom 13:7a*

The word custom comes from *telos*, which refers to, "a duty, a toll," or, as we would understand it, a custom [fee] paid on goods that are being transported.[27]

> *...fear to whom fear 13:7b*

The word *fear* refers to, "respect or courtesy."

...honor to whom honor. 13:7c

The word *timen*, which is translated "honor," is used. It means, "to pay the esteem due to one in authority or leadership."

Don't miss the truth that this list of duties represents not only our *action* but our *attitude*.[28]

———

APPLICATION

Paying taxes to the offices of government is worthy.

Because paying taxes is commanded by God and is the privilege of the believer, you can take pleasure in it. When April rolls around, just remember that paying taxes is the will of God, and obedience to the will of God is action that will one day be *rewarded* by Christ at the Bema Seat. Imagine—you will one day be rewarded for paying your taxes. Think of it as the ultimate tax refund!

However, there are rewards, even now; take note the next time you hike or camp in a national park, enjoy food inspected by our national food system, walk down a busy hallway and trust the center for infectious diseases to do their governmental task, enjoy the city library, have an emergency in which you need to call the police or firefighters to your home, or take your sixteen-year-old son to get his driver's license! Take pleasure in the fact that as you obeyed God, you contributed to these and a thousand other benefits within this culture *because* you paid your taxes.

Acting graciously to the officials of government is a winsome witness.

The attitude in which we support our government brings either honor or dishonor to the cause of Christ. Listen to Justin Martyr, who lived in the midst of tremendous persecution in the first century, as he wrote to his political leaders:

> Everywhere we, more readily than all men, endeavor to pay to those appointed by you the taxes, both ordinary and extraordinary, as we have been taught by Jesus Christ. We worship only God, but in other things we will gladly serve you, acknowledging you as kings and rulers of men, and praying that, with your kingly power, you [will have] sound judgment.[29]

Wow! What a witness for Christ; with quiet dignity and great theology he testified that God alone is sovereign.

How do we live with the spirit and attitude of Justin Martyr? By pledging allegiance to the divine Emperor, and the government which is upon His shoulders, whose kingdom is unparalleled and eternal. Remember, you are headed for His Empire!

CONCLUSION

While preaching in London, England in 1862, Charles Spurgeon encouraged his congregation; "Let us remember that we are simply passing through this earth, and should bless it in our transit, but never yoke ourselves to its affairs. It is passing away. We are as British subjects living for a while in Spain…knowing that we will soon be traveling home."[30]

What a wonderful truth. This city, this nation, this planet is not our home. So what is this home like?

> *[There is] a river of the water of life, clear as crystal, coming from the throne of God and of the Lamb,*
>
> *²in the middle of its street. On either side of the river was the tree of life, bearing twelve kinds of fruit, yielding its fruit every month.*
>
> *³There will no longer be any curse; and the throne of God and of the Lamb will be in it, and His bond-servants will serve Him;*

⁴they shall see His face, and His name will be on their foreheads.

⁵And there will no longer be any night; and they will not have need of the light of a lamp nor the light of the sun, because the Lord God will illumine them; and they will reign forever and ever.

⁷And behold, I am coming quickly. (Revelation 22:1–5, 7)

We, who long for that eternal country; that kingdom of justice and joy, goodness and grace, say, "Even so, come, Lord Jesus." Come now! But until You do, we shall bless earth with holy lives as we journey through it as worthy citizens and as diligent witnesses to the glory and honor of Your name—

> *King of Kings,*
> *Emperor of Emperors,*
> *President of Presidents,*
> *Caesar of Caesars,*
> *Lord of Lords!*

Unto You, we pledge our ultimate and final allegiance.

FURTHER QUESTIONS

Are you saying Christians shouldn't vote?

Enjoying the benefits of a free society requires a sense of responsibility to serve and act as a good citizen. I agree with Daniel Webster who wrote, "Whatever makes good Christians, makes good citizens." Exercising the privileges of a free society should be used to our advantage whenever possible. Even the Apostle Paul exercised his right as a Roman citizen—it kept him from receiving a beating by the authorities (Acts 22:25). I must add, however, Paul never made it his *mission* to stamp out beatings or to protect the rights of Roman citizenship.

So vote. And vote intelligently. In order to vote for the best candidate, gather all the information available. Voter guides, internet research, and other sources of public record concerning the candidate's position, views, and voting record should be examined. Too often the candidates are both immoral and anti-God. In that case you might have to vote for the "lesser evil." As you vote, remember that the heart of the king is in the hand of God (Proverbs 21:1), and God is sovereign over every decision, judgment, and policy.

What is your opinion of Christians serving in the political arena?

The political arena is a wonderful place for committed Christians to shine for God's glory. In the Old Testament, several key individuals (Nehemiah and Daniel) served their political leaders with dignity and godliness. Daniel so effectively shone as a light in the darkness that two of the kings he served placed their faith in God. Daniel's godly influence was still felt, centuries later, as men from his former office (Magi) traveled from Daniel's homeland to worship the Messiah.

Furthermore, there were committed believers serving in Caesar's household during the early days of the church (Philippians 4:22). In addition, there were judges and civil servants also following Christ—whose jobs didn't end the moment they became followers of Christ!

As with any profession, Christians are salt and light. Though we should not be any profession that requires us to leave our testimony in the lobby, our role in any other profession is to create thirst for the truth of Scripture, and our testimony should inhibit the rapid decay around us. By our character, we expose the deeds of darkness and shine the light of Christ's beauty into the longing eyes of blinded people. Politicians with a testimony for holy living and biblical thinking are rare—but greatly appreciated as they stand for the truth of God's Word.

One of the unfortunate things in the pluralistic quagmire of our culture is the continual attempt to dampen the clear testimony of political leaders. Unfortunately, many political figures give in. Suddenly, any talk of belief in Jesus Christ becomes "faith in God." Salvation is neutered to "my strong belief in God."

My hope is that Christians will retain their clear mission in whatever field of service they pursue. They are Christians first, and politicians, doctors, students, mechanics, secretaries, and lawyers second.

Aren't you arguing from silence? Just because Paul doesn't mention political activism, how do you know it isn't the thing for Christians to do?

You're right, the New Testament epistles are silent; God's revelation to the church is mute on the issue.

I think silence is unimportant when the issue is unimportant. The Bible doesn't mention pianos, potlucks, and pastoral sabbaticals, but I'm for all three!

However, this issue of the mission of the church, as well as the individual believer, is not an unimportant issue. Therefore, if the Lord wanted us to engage our culture in a war, wouldn't He have given us some instructions? Wouldn't there be at least one example in either Paul's or Peter's letters to the church?

Silence can be deafening.

In this case, the mission of the church is not a silent issue. We have hundreds of verses indicating the behavior and activity of the believer in the world today.

Not to mention the great commission of our Lord— the mission of the church—to be His witnesses; to be His ambassadors; to urge our world to be reconciled to God.

This is our mission…and the Bible is anything but silent!

Should the Christian boycott companies and products promoting sinful activities?

Certainly, an industry that directly practices immorality should be avoided, such as casinos or strip clubs. The greater difficulty lies in boycotting companies that indirectly promote sinful behavior. The United States Government, for instance, allocates money for immoral art displays. Would boycotting include a refusal to pay taxes to the government? Some Christians believe so.

There are many other difficult issues. What about helping an unmarried woman feed her children, or going to a specialist whose clinic donates money to birth control measures overseas? Don't forget purchasing gasoline at a station which sells pornographic magazines, and eating at a restaurant that sells alcoholic beverages or plays ungodly music over the speaker system. There's also the problem of buying a newspaper that donates proceeds to liberal causes, or paying city taxes which in turn support same-sex advocacy programs.

And that's just the beginning!

My opinion is that Christians should refuse to subsidize direct involvement with any sinful behavior. As it relates to indirect subsidy, I merely applaud any Christian who tries to be consistent with their lives. However, I am concerned when Christians publicly boycott a company, store, or product which only has indirect involvement with sinful issues. It is easy to be misunderstood by the unbelieving world. They can easily get the wrong message—that we care more about their sinful behavior than we do their soul.

Our greatest concern revolves around the world hearing the gospel, not an attempt to make unbelieving men stop going to strip bars, selling porn magazines in their stores, or spending their profit to underwrite the deeds of darkness.

If anyone had the right to encourage believers to stop paying taxes, it was the Apostle Paul; for it would be those taxes which would ultimately subsidize the games, where Christians would pay the ultimate sacrifice. Yet, knowing full well the wickedness of the government, he commanded believers to pay their taxes.

Is it ever right to speak out on issues we find offensive?

Absolutely! As we've already learned, John Knox of Scotland dared to challenge Queen Mary. Before him, John the Baptist, challenged Herod for his immorality (Mark 6:18).

What's needful is the correct context of our comments. We may clearly share our grief over the issue at hand, but we must share why it is grievous to us. It is because the acts of sin are dishonorable to our true and living God. It is because those acts slander the glory of God in His creation. It is because our bodies, His highest creation, are dishonored and ruined by sin. This is the context of our offense. If we merely speak of our offenses, the world will view us as any other voter who isn't happy when things don't go his way. But if our comments are attached to a kind, clear message of the gospel, God's work will be advanced.

We are not called by God to curse the darkness. We are called to simply shine…and the darker our culture, the brighter our light.

We are commanded in Romans 12:21 to overcome evil with good. Isn't that what the Christian coalitions and the "religious right" are attempting to do?

This argument is based on a faulty interpretation of this text. The idea of gaining victory (*nikaw*) over evil does not mean that evil is eliminated. In fact, the prior verses say as much. The believer is to feed and clothe and help the unbeliever start their stove fire after it's gone out. Heaping coals of fire on their head was a literal act! It wasn't a reference to judgment, or some form of scolding. It literally meant to give your neighbor some hot coals from your fire and pile them on the platter your neighbor would then balance on his head as he walked back to his home to re-start his own fire. What an act of kindness!

Do the sinners in our culture believe they are the enemy of the church? I believe so! Paul would encourage us to so live that our unbelieving world is graced by our holy lives, startled by our gracious response to injury, and mystified by our *loving* reproach of sin.

Does America's moral decline mean
God has abandoned us?

The invitation to America is not a national invitation. Our invitation is to *people* within every nation. Americans are not God's "people," nor is this country under some special covenant with God. Sermons and speeches about "reclaiming America for God" may sound wonderful, but they give false hope to Americans. Worse yet, they misdirect the energy and focus of the church. Our mission is not to save America, but to save Americans—that is, to share the gospel of grace to people who need deliverance.

God hasn't abandoned America anymore than He abandoned the land of the Ninevites. At the very height of their immorality and wickedness, God had plans for them through a prophet by the name of Jonah. Today, the invitation of the gospel is for everyone—and certainly this nation of people. And according to Scripture, the invitation is still open! We are still living in the days of "whosoever will, may come." At the end of human history, as we know it, humanity will be divided into two camps. D. L. Moody used to call these two camps, the "whosoever wills" and the "whosoever won'ts."

Our mission as believers is not based upon national renewal, but individual salvation. I believe it is easy for Christians to talk about winning the culture war, all the while never sharing Christ with their neighbor. It's a lot easier to pray for my congressman to make the right decision than it is to help my next door neighbor understand the claims of Christ. In fact, it's easier to talk of national sin, than deal with personal sin.

While we never hear the Apostle Paul refer to the gross immoralities of Nero—and there were many!—Paul repeatedly challenged the believer to live a pure and holy life. He knew that holy believers were the best advertisements for the life-changing gospel of Christ.

By the way, according to Paul's sermon to the proud Athenians, God has already mapped out our country's appointed times, borders, and national destiny (Acts 17:26). How long we exist as a nation; where our borders lie; the nature of our leadership; and the future of our country are His issues. The state of this union is actually in the hands of God!

ENDNOTES

ENDNOTES

[1] Erwin Lutzer, *Where Do We Go From Here?* (Moody Press, 1993), p. 25.

[2] Erwin Lutzer, *Why the Cross Can Do What Politics Can't* (Harvest House, 1999), p. 11.

[3] Kevin Bauder, *In the Nick of Time* (2005).

[4] John MacArthur, *Romans* (Moody Press, 1994), p. 210.

[5] Lutzer, *Politics*, p. 47.

[6] Ibid., p. 40.

[7] Ibid., p. 47.

[8] James Montgomery Boice, *Two Cities, Two Loves* (Intervarsity Press, 1996), p. 168.

[9] John MacArthur, *Fool's Gold: Discerning Truth in an Age of Error* (Crossway Books, 2005), p. 147.

[10] Boice, p. 182.

[11] Roy L. Laurin, *Romans: Where Life Begins* (Kregel, 1948), p. 435.

[12] Alva J. McClain, *Romans: The Gospel of God's Grace* (BMH Books, 1973), p. 221.

[13] Boice, p. 198.

[14] Newsweek (Mar. 29, 1999), p. 60.

[15] C. S. Lewis, *Mere Christianity* (HarperCollins, 2001 *reprint*), p. 134–135.

[16] New York Times (Mar. 1998).

[17] Ed Dobson and Cal Thomas, *Blinded By Might* (Zondervan, 1999), back cover.

[18] Erwin Lutzer, *Twelve Myths Americans Believe* (Moody Press, 1993), p. 181.

[19] Dobson and Thomas, p. 112.

[20] John MacArthur, *Why Government Can't Save You* (Word Publishing, 2000), p. 42.

[21] Ibid., p. 46.

[22] Ibid., p. 45.

[23] Ibid., p. 54.

[24] Woodrow Kroll, *Romans: Righteousness in Christ* (AMG Publishers, 2002), p. 212.

[25] Joey Adams, *Christian Reader*, vol. 32, no. 3.

[26] Jim George, *God's Man of Influence* (Harvest House Publishers, 2003).

[27] Fritz Rienecker, *Linguistic Key to the Greek New Testament* (Zondervan, 1980), p. 378.

[28] Kroll, p. 212.

[29] R. Kent Hughes, *Romans* (Crossway Books, 1991), p. 245.

[30] MacArthur, *Government*, p. 147.

WISDOM FOR THE HEART

WHAT IS WISDOM FOR THE HEART?

Wisdom for the Heart is an international Bible-teaching ministry based on the sermons of Dr. Stephen Davey. Heard throughout the world, this radio ministry is unique because it brings listeners through the Bible book-by-book, verse-by-verse, sometimes word-by-word!

Stephen encourages believers to live holy lives for the Lord Jesus Christ through the timeless, timely, life-changing Word of God. Join us as we worship and praise the living Word, the Lord Jesus Christ. Life's truest meaning can only be found revealed in the Scriptures alone.

Check out **www.wisdomonline.org** to find out if Wisdom for the Heart can be heard in your city.

More Stephen Davey books are available

at www.wisdomonline.org and in your Christian bookstore.

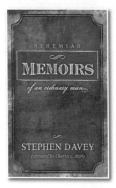

Nehemiah

Nehemiah probably wouldn't have wanted the spotlight shone on him, but that's not to say he wouldn't have deserved it. The life of Nehemiah will inspire you to serve the faithful God he served with so much resolve. You will be awed by the God who led Nehemiah to attempt amazing things for His glory.

> *"Stephen Davey always has one eye on the text of Scripture, and the other on us as he brings the story of Nehemiah across the centuries into our lives and hearts."* Dr. Erwin W. Lutzer, Senior Pastor, Moody Church

> *"Thoroughly biblical and relevant to a 21st century context, this book will be a great encouragement to all who turn its pages."* Dr. Daniel L. Akin, President, Southeastern Baptist Theological Seminary

Ruth

Hidden in the pages of the Old Testament is the beautiful story of love and redemption between a wealthy landowner and a poor widow. The story of Ruth and Boaz, carefully explained by Stephen Davey, author of *Nehemiah: Memoirs of an Ordinary Man*, will dazzle the imagination and ignite the emotions.

Walk beneath the shadows of despair as Ruth and Naomi eek out an existence by foraging for leftover grain. Feel the emotions of Boaz as he carefully protects Ruth while secretly yearning for her affections. Watch in amazement as the sovereign hand of God is revealed in making this fairytale come true.

WISDOM FOR THE HEART

www.wisdomonline.org

1-866-48-BIBLE

SHEPHERDS
THEOLOGICAL SEMINARY

There is an undeniable privilege of learning how to be a shepherd from someone who wears the fragrance of sheep, someone who knows how to use a shepherd's staff. In fact, there's nothing quite like a professor with a few splinters in his hands, a teacher who knows the pain and pleasure of serving the Lord in the pastureland of ministry. At Shepherds Theological Seminary, students will learn from those who practice on Sunday what they teach on Monday.

Degrees Offered

Master of Divinity
Master of Arts in Pastoral Ministry
Master of Arts in Biblical Counseling
Master of Arts in Biblical Literature
Master of Arts in Christian Education

Shepherds Theological Seminary is currently housed on the beautiful campus of Colonial Baptist Church in Cary, North Carolina, a short driving distance from Raleigh, Chapel Hill, and Durham.

www.ShepherdsSeminary.org
info@ShepherdsSeminary.org
(800) 672-3060